Sunday $pending Instead of Sunday Giving

God's Resources

Kevin L. Cann

Litchfield, IL 62056
http://www.revivalwavesofglory.com

Sunday $pending Instead of Sunday Giving

© 2013 by Kevin Cann
All rights reserved. No part of this book may be reproduced, stored in a retrieval system or transmitted in any form or by any means without the prior written permission of the publishers, except by a reviewer who may quote brief passages in a review to be printed in a newspaper, magazine or journal.

1st Printing

Publisher has allowed this work to remain exactly as the author intended, verbatim, without editorial input.

Unless otherwise indicated, all Scripture quotations are taken from *The Holy Bible, New King James Version.* Copyright © 1979, 1980, 1982 by Thomas Nelson, Inc.

Ebook 978-1-312-04484-5

Softcover 978-1-312-04481-4

Hardcover 978-1-312-04482-1

PUBLISHED BY REVIVAL WAVES OF GLORY BOOKS & PUBLISHING
www.revivalwavesofglory.com
Litchfield, IL

Printed in the United States of America

Table of Contents

Dedication 5
Introduction 7
Chapter 1 Needs 9
Chapter 2 Wants 15
Chapter 3 Assets 21
Chapter 4 Liabilities 27
Chapter 5 Net Worth 31
Chapter 6 Good/Bad Debt 35
Chapter 7 $ Working for You 39
Chapter 8 You Working for $ 43
Chapter 9 Sabbath Day 45
Chapter 10 Tithing 49
Kingdom Financial Plan 53
Contact the Author 63
Other Products Available 65

Sunday $pending Instead of Sunday Giving

Dedication

I would like to dedicate this book to my Heavenly Father. He gave me the words to put in this book. This book would not be possible without the help of the Holy Spirit giving me guidance and direction. I am thankful to Jesus Christ for saving me from my sins. I thank all three from the bottom of my heart.

I would also like to dedicate this book to my beautiful wife, Bethany. She has helped me get out of my comfort zone and become a finisher. She is the encouragement I need in my life. I love you.

Sunday $pending Instead of Sunday Giving

Introduction

This is my third book. God gave me this title as my wife and I were leaving a premium outlet mall in St. Louis, MO. It was a beautiful Sunday afternoon and we decided to go check out this new outlet mall. We could hardly find a parking spot the place was so packed. As we walked around the outdoor style mall, I could not believe all the people there spending money. I'm a very conservative person but this place just seemed as though people were on a spending frenzy. I'm sure there were people who could afford to spend some money that day and it not affect their lifestyle. I also believe there was people spending money they didn't have to spend. In other words, they were going into debt to buy things.

We are now entering the biggest spending season of the year. As I write this, Thanksgiving is over and the Christmas shopping season has begun. It was hard for me to imagine that the stores opened even earlier this year. If we continue this trend, there will not even be a Happy Thanksgiving. We are supposed to be thankful for what God has done for us. Society is trying to replace that with spending money on things that we don't need. I am not against shopping for Christmas presents for friends and family, but to stand in line for hours to save some money is CRAZY. God is our provider not Wal-Mart. I hope to provide a new perspective on managing God's money. Not according to the world. This will be based upon the Kingdom of God. God is trying to get my wife and I to switch from "natural resources" to the "supernatural resources" of heaven. I pray our eyes can be opened to what heaven has in store for all of us. I encourage you to read "Who is Your $ource" before reading this book. It will give you a good understanding of Who your source is before learning how to manage those resources. God Bless!

Chapter 1

Needs

Everyone has *needs*. Also, everyone's *needs* are different. The definition of *needs*: as a verb, require (something) because it is essential or very important. Now let's look at some noun definitions: 1. Circumstances in which something is necessary, or that require some course of action; necessity. 2. A thing that is wanted or required. 3. The state of requiring help, or lacking basic necessities such as food.

As a society, we began to distort what are *real* needs and what are *wants*. My wife and I have discovered in our first year of marriage that we have some very basic *needs*. We both lost our jobs shortly after we got back from our honeymoon. This opportunity to grow in God has been amazing and a little challenging. Our needs are pretty basic: food, shelter, and clothing, gas for the vehicles and occasional spending money for a movie. Now I know you might be saying, "Wow! Like you are really roughing it!" Well, we live off of payments that come in from properties that I bought and rehabbed years ago. The payments are not enough to pay the expenses on the properties and support us. As I write this book, we have so many bills unpaid. We are driving around a car with plates that have been expired for 6 months… (Don't let the police know).

    I am so grateful to my heavenly Father for providing everything that we *actually* need. We both have learned that we have it very good. We don't have to wake up each day and go work for someone else. God always shows up right on time for us. I remember several times when we needed money to pay a bill or buy some food and He would provide the resources somehow. One time my brother called and said he had a heating and cooling job and needed some help. I worked with him and received pay immediately. I remembered needing money for food one day and then I received a rental payment from one of the properties. Another time, one of the renters paid me early. Let me tell you that *never* happens. God uses all kinds of different ways to get resources to us.

    In Isaiah 55:8 "For My thoughts are not your thoughts, nor are your ways My ways, "says the Lord. We have been so used to getting our needs met by working at our jobs and now God was showing us how *He* can meet our *needs* without a job. I remember recently how we had a big property insurance bill was due. I had been trying to sell a trailer for some time. Then, this older gentleman calls me on the phone and would like to take a look at it. He ends up buying the trailer that day. The funny thing he told me was that every time he would call about another trailer, it would be sold! God has his ways. Bethany and I went out to eat that night. We both really appreciated that meal. It had been awhile since we were able to treat ourselves to dining out. I think that steak tasted better than all the other ones I had ever eaten.

Now, this might not sound like a big deal to some people. I realize that in third world countries kids don't even have shelter, food, water or clothing. Each person has a different level of *needs*. The important part is to be thankful for everything we have and not upset about the things we don't have. My wife and I are very grateful for the duplex that we currently live in. It meets our *needs* at this time in our life. That doesn't mean that we don't *want* a house of our own. My wife has waited so very long to have a house of her own, she dreams about decorating it. We already have a certain house in mind. This house she desires is not a *need* at this time, it's a *want* item. We are not going to go buy the house just because we *want* it. That is the viewpoint out there for some people. This is one reason we ended up with a real estate bubble. Banks were lending to anyone and people were buying *wants* instead of *need* items. I don't believe there is anything wrong with buying a big home. My wife and I have big plans for our first home. The important lesson that we can all learn is to buy things when it's the right time. The right time is in God's timing, not our own. This can be difficult to understand. We are currently learning to listen to the Holy

Spirit and follow His lead. I am using our future home as an example but this can apply to anything.

We currently don't have the income to purchase this dream home. We are trusting in God that He will provide the resources at the right time. God does *want* to give you the desires of your heart. In Psalms 37:4-5 it states: "Delight yourself also in the Lord, and He shall give you the desires of your heart. Commit your way to the Lord, trust also in Him and He shall bring it to pass." The problem we create as humans is trying to help God with our desires. Sometimes *we* make decisions that are based on *our* desires and then we *want* God to bless it. God does not work like that. We have to trust Him and let Him do the work. After all He did create the world in one week. Anything else He does is no problem for Him at all.

My main point to this first chapter is to first understand that each and every one of us has different *needs*. We also need to keep in mind that *God* is our provider. In Philippians 4:19 "And my God shall supply all your need according to His riches and in glory by Christ Jesus". Most people have heard this scripture in church. The real issue is: do we as believers of Christ trust in him to fulfill this promise? As I write this I am being challenged by my flesh to question this promise. One thing that I have realized is that the flesh does not like the principals of the Kingdom of God. The reason is very simple, yet hard to overcome. It's all about who is in control. The flesh *wants* to be in control but God *needs* to be in control of our lives. The *wants* are controlled by emotions. *Needs* are controlled by the Spirit. We all have *needs* in life and the only One who can meet our every *need* is our Heavenly Father. Our Father in heaven will always take care of His children. God is good.

As my wife and I were going to the bank to deposit a check for her health insurance(an expense we really didn't have the extra income for), we saw a car pull in front of us that had "gd prvd" on the license plate. We believed the abbreviation stood for "God provides". This was God getting my attention. At that very moment we were spending money we didn't have to spend. My flesh was not happy about spending this money on health insurance. I thought "we have other bills to pay with this money". God was just reminding me that He is in control, not me. I don't know how He is going to get the money to us to pay these bills. I just trust in Him that He will provide. What a lesson I learned that day. God has His ways of doing things that are completely different than our ways. It is hard to adjust to living a "supernatural" lifestyle but it is much better than living a normal "natural" lifestyle.

Sunday $pending Instead of Sunday Giving

Chapter 2

Wants

We all have *wants*. The definition of *wants* in the verb form is as follows: 1. Have a desire to possess or do (something); wish for. 2. Lack or be short of something desirable or essential. Now the noun definitions: 1. A lack or deficiency of something. 2. A desire for something.

If you notice, the word "desire" shows up in several of these definitions. God *wants* to give us the desires of our hearts. In Psalms 37:4-5 "Delight yourself also in the Lord, and he shall give you the desires of your heart. Commit your way to the Lord, trust also in Him, and He shall bring it to pass". The key to the verse is to delight ourselves in the Lord, commit our ways to Him and trust in Him. *Wants* are not evil. The problem with most of us is that we put our *wants* above God. Our *wants* become our god. This is what usually happens when society tries to acquire items on their own instead of waiting on God.

This is what causes people to be shopaholics, hoarders, substance abusers, etc. They are all trying to fill a void in their lives. We all have a wanting of something.

That something can only be filled or satisfied by Jesus Christ. He is the only answer to this problem. Once we have accepted Him as our Lord and Savior, then He can begin to fill that void that we have in our lives. I know from experience because I was an alcoholic. I tried to use alcohol as my solution to my problems. In the end, Jesus is the only one who can help me. If we try to acquire our *wants* without Jesus, trouble will ensue shortly afterwords.

This is one reason why people get into debt: they are trying to fill a void by buying things. Since I am focusing on money management in this book, we will talk about this subject most of the time. It's important to have a budget in place. This will teach us discipline. When emotions are in control, there is no discipline.

God expects us to be good stewards of His resources. In Matthew 25:14-21, 24-30 reads: "For the kingdom of heaven is like a man traveling to a far country, who called his own servants and delivered his goods to them. And to one he gave five talents, to another two, and to another one, to each according to his own ability; and immediately he went on a journey. Then he who had received the five talents went and traded with them, and made another five talents. And likewise he who had received two gained two more also. But he who had received one went and dug in the ground, and hid his lord's money. After a long time the lord of those servants came and settled accounts with them. So he who had received five talents came and brought five other talents, saying,

'Lord you delivered to me five talents; look, I have gained five more talents besides them.' His lord said to him, 'Well done, good and faithful servant; you were faithful over a few things, I will make you ruler over many things. Enter into the joy of your lord.' Then he who had received the one talent came and said, 'Lord, I knew you to be a hard man, reaping where you have not sown, and gathering where you have not scattered seed. And I was afraid, and went and hid your talent in the ground. Look, there you have what is yours.' But his lord answered and said to him, 'You wicked and lazy servant, you knew that I reap where I have not sown, and gather where I have not scattered seed. So you ought to have deposited my money with the bankers, and at my coming I would have received back my own with interest. Therefore take the talent from him, and give it to him who has ten talents. For to everyone who has, more will be given, and he will have abundance; but from him who does not have, even what he has will be taken away. And cast the unprofitable servant into the outer darkness. There will be weeping and gnashing of teeth."

The important thing to remember about *wants* is to not let them have control of your life. God is the only One who should have control of our lives. It is important for us to exalt Him. There are many things in this world that could be put in place of God: Money, fame, material things, sex, people, etc. I always believed that I could have my cake and eat it too. As long as we keep God first in our lives, we can still enjoy the other things of life too. A lot of people trip up when they forget about God after He has blessed them. My goal is to never forget that God gives me everything and that He can take it all away too. In Job 1:20-21 "Then Job arose, tore his robe, and shaved his head; and he fell to the ground and worshiped. And he said: "Naked I came from my mother's womb, and naked shall I return there. The Lord gave, and the Lord has taken away; Blessed be the name of the Lord." He is a good God and He *wants* us to worship Him first. God does not have a problem with us enjoying the finer things in life. After all, He did create everything. He is looking at our heart.

In Luke 15"11-21 "Then He said: "A certain man had two sons. And the younger of them said to his father, 'Father, give me the portion of goods that falls to me.' So he divided to them his livelihood. And not many days after, the younger son gathered all together, journeyed to a far country, and there wasted his possessions with prodigal living. But when he had spent all, there arose a severe famine in that land and he began to be in want. Then he went and joined himself to a citizen of that country, and he sent him into his fields to feed swine. And he would gladly have filled his stomach with the pods that the swine ate, and no one gave him anything. But when he came to himself, he said, 'How many of my father's hired servants have bread enough and to spare, and I perish with hunger! 'I will arise and go to my father, and will say to him, "Father, I have sinned against heaven and before you, and I am no longer worthy to be called your son. Make me like one of your hired servants." And he arose and came to his father. But when he was still a great way off, his father saw him and had compassion, and ran and fell on his neck and kissed him."

God just *wants* us to put Him first in our lives. If we can do that *and* remain humble, He will bless us with the gifts we *want* in our lives. This seems like a real simple principle, but it is much more difficult to walk out. My wife and I are at a place in our lives were we are walking this principle out as I write this book. I must admit, it is much harder to walk it out than to write about it. We know God will give us the strength we need to transition through this season. One way He gives us hope and encouragement is through prophetic words. I am a big believer in the prophetic voice. I am very thankful that we have several prophetic voices speaking into our lives. We have to see the future in order to endure the present. God has an amazing plan for our lives here on planet earth and He *wants* us to fulfill our destiny.

In Matthew 6:25-33 "Therefore I say to you, do not **worry** about your life, what you will eat or what you will drink; nor about your body, what you will put on. Is not life more than food and the body more than clothing? "Look at the birds of the air, for they neither sow nor reap nor gather into barns; yet your heavenly Father feeds them. Are you not of more value than they? "Which of you by worrying can add one cubit to his stature? "So why do you worry about clothing? Consider the lilies of the field, how they grow: they never toil nor spin; and yet I say to you that even Solomon in all his glory was not arrayed like one of these. "Now if God so clothes the grass of the field, which today is, and tomorrow is thrown into the oven, will He not much more clothe you, O you of little faith? "Therefore do not worry, saying, 'What shall we eat? Or 'What shall we drink?' or 'What shall we wear?' "For after all these things the Gentiles seek. For your heavenly Father knows that you need all these things. "But seek first the kingdom of God and His righteousness, and all these things shall be added to you."

Chapter 3

Assets

What is an *asset*? An *asset* is any items of economic value owned by an individual or corporation, especially that which could be converted to cash. The most valuable *asset* is cash. The old saying, "Cash is king" is a real valuable *asset*. The reason cash is a valuable *asset* is because our economic system is based upon it. Let's use for example a personal experience that my wife and I had when trying to purchase a home. We went to the bank and received a pre-approval letter to make an offer on a home. We made a very **strong** offer on the home. Someone else made a strong offer on the home as well, but it was all cash. Our offer was a loan with contingencies. The seller had no problem taking the all cash offer. Other *assets* would include: retirement fund, real estate, stocks and bonds. If your car or truck is paid for it would also be considered an *asset*.

I would like to talk about a misconception in the accounting world with regards to *assets*. I will use a personal example to explain this misconception. I have a real estate business that buys and sells property. We also rent out property. I decided that I could use some equipment to help us work on the properties. So I went out and bought a dump truck, skid steer, trailers, box truck and a mini excavator. I bought all this equipment with cash. On the accounting books these are all listed as *assets*. The real problem is that I have just tied up the most valuable *asset*: cash. I was thinking that having this equipment around would help my business but it only hurt the business. Not only is my cash sitting around in the equipment while not in use but it also costs money to maintain them. So what I really created was a *liability* for my company. Of course I was able to sell off the equipment for cash but I still had the *liability* of the cash being tied up during the ownership of the equipment. From a financial perspective, cash flow is the heartbeat of a household or business.

    I also purchased some vacant lots and houses to rehab. These properties also appear on an *asset* sheet. Since I purchased these properties, I have had to maintain them by cutting the grass and other minor things. I have also had to pay the real estate taxes and property insurance on these properties. Once again I found myself with cash going out of the company instead of in the company. I believe I had good intentions by purchasing these properties. I have sold two vacant lots and made some good money. The problem is that my profits get used up by all the expenses of the other properties. It is important to have a game plan on what to do with properties before we buy them. I also got carried away and purchased too many at one time. It is better to purchase one house at a time. So now I have multiple houses sitting and costing me money. That turns my *assets* into *liabilities*. I should have finished the last one I was working on before I purchased anymore. My problem would be that the properties available for sale were such a great buy for me. I couldn't resist passing up a great deal.

Now I'm going to shock a lot of people with this misconception. We are all taught that our home is our greatest *asset* that we purchase in our lifetime. I do agree with the fact that a house can be liquidated for cash. My problem with a home as an *asset* is from the cash flow analysis. We purchase a home and pay each month: mortgage, real estate taxes, insurance, utilities, water, and trash bills. This is a lot of cash flow going out and no cash flow coming into your home. Think of your home as a business; cash flow going out and nothing coming in equals bankruptcy. Now we all know that the payoff with a home is when we sell it. We all know what happened to the people who could not sell their homes in the recent real estate bubble. I would like people to think differently about purchasing a home.

I would like to give you a personal example: my wife and I are living in a duplex that we own. The mortgage is covered by the renter on the other side. So we have cash flow coming in to cover **some** of the cash flow going out. Of course not everyone wants to live in a duplex. We are living in this temporarily, until we have the cash flow to purchase our dream home. We are going to use the home to run several businesses. This will give us the cash flow we need to pay the bills on this home purchase. By purchasing a larger home than what we need and using the extra space for businesses, we will not need to rent office space. So we will take the money we would use for rent and pay our mortgage with it. To me this is a true *asset*. Our home is *producing* cash instead of *taking* cash.

    The next *asset* I would like to talk about is retirement funds. This is the last *asset* we should ever want to liquidate. As I am writing this book my wife and I chose to liquidate our retirement funds. I do not recommend doing this unless it is necessary. We are using ours to pay bills that we have accumulated during our *transition* from regular jobs to *God ideas*. For more on *God ideas* you can read it in my book "God Idea vs. Good Idea".

    Our retirement fund is a great *asset* for many things. It is important to keep cash going into this account every year. We are allowed to borrow from this account. We can also use it to purchase real estate. The problem with my wife and me liquidating our accounts is time. Now we will have to put even more money back into the accounts to get us back on track. We believe through different business ventures that we can produce enough cash flow to replace our balances and get us back were we need to be for the future. It is very important to start early in life. The sooner we start saving, the better off we will be later on in life. Also if we start at a young age we can take advantage of higher returns with stocks instead of bonds.

Stocks are a great *asset*. They are very liquid *assets*. The biggest problem that I encounter with stocks is the timing of liquidation. If you have to get out for any reason at all you will have to take the current price. That can be a bad situation depending on the condition of the market. My advice is to get out when you *want* to get out instead of when you *need* to get out. In order to do that you will have to put yourself in a situation where you do not *need* any of the money you have invested in the stock market. This will require good **money** management. I hope this book will help many people understand Kingdom principles pertaining to money management so they can put themselves into a greater position to prosper. In John 3:2 "Beloved, I pray that you may prosper in all things and be in good health, just as your soul prospers".

Sunday $pending Instead of Sunday Giving

Chapter 4

Liabilities

A *liability* is any financial obligations, debts, claims, or potential losses. Most people know the basic *liabilities*: mortgage, auto loans, credit cards, student loans, etc. Unsecured *liabilities* are the worse. Credit cards fall into this category. I personally have a lot of unsecured debt. This happened through a few different series of events. Just like most things in life, it does not happen overnight. It usually takes some time to accumulate a lot of unsecured debt.

Part of my unsecured debt came from an investment that I made in Ford stock. I didn't have any cash to invest when Ford went down to $2 or less a share. So I used my credit cards with cash advances to acquire the cash necessary to invest. If I *would* have paid the credit cards off when I cashed out of Ford, then everything would have been fine. I chose to continue giving into the Kingdom of God instead of paying off the debt. This was a *personal* choice.

Also I had a real estate transaction that left a lot of unsecured debt. I used the credit cards to purchase materials for a home. The property I had just finished did not come in at the value I was expecting. This value affected my borrowing power which in turn made it difficult for me to pay off the unsecured debt. As you can see it only takes a few mistakes and you can find yourself a slave to debt.

Most people that go to college come out of school with student loans to pay off. I was no different than most graduates. I did have the good fortune of having my student loan paid as part of my salary when I started my first job after graduation. I know most people don't have this opportunity but it is important to keep in mind that you will inherit this *liability* at graduation.

Auto loans are a huge *liability* in America. We are in love with our cars. I must admit that I am no different. When I graduated from college, the first purchase I made was a motorcycle, then, my second purchase was a mustang. I felt this was a good reward for graduating college. Looking back I would have kept driving the company truck and saved the money I spent on these purchases. The problem with purchasing most vehicles is that it is a depreciating *asset*. That means its value is going down each day. In reality it is a *liability*.

I will give you a personal example: I purchased a used BMW for cash. The good part is I did not have a loan against it but I sold the car two years later for half of what I paid for it. The value of the car had fallen *that* much. If I would have had a loan against the car it would have been even worse. The bottom line is that cars, trucks, boats, motorcycles are really *liabilities* not *assets*. The best way to purchase a vehicle is with cash and below market value. I would also recommend a good used vehicle instead of a brand new one.

When purchasing items that depreciate, always keep in mind what you think it would bring in the market place should you have to liquidate down the road for some reason or another. Try to plan for the unexpected. This will help keep your emotions in check during purchases. This can prevent you from overpaying. Overpaying is usually what gets most people in over their heads.

There are times when tough decisions have to be made with our finances. I am a firm believer in paying my bills on time. Recently, we had to make some hard decisions in regard to our finances. My wife and I decided to stop paying some unsecured debt (credit cards) because we had some secured debt that we had to keep paying or we would risk losing properties. It is always better to pay secured debt first. I pray anyone reading this book does not have to make the choice we did. We are putting our trust in God that He will correct any damage that may come as a result of this decision. Our credit score could be affected by not paying these bills. The credit score system is a man-made system. The Kingdom system does not have credit scores. The Kingdom system is about sowing and reaping.

My wife and I have done a lot of sowing, so we believe we will reap a harvest, it's just a matter of time.

God has us in a "test" season. He is transitioning us from reliance on natural incomes, like our jobs, to supernatural incomes. I do not encourage readers to engage in this journey on their own accord. Please, be led by the Holy Spirit.

My flesh does not like me being late with these bills. I get 7-10 calls a day from creditors. I do not answer, because I don't want to give in to the stress that the creditors will put on me. I began to realize the bondage I was under by this debt. I am actually set free from it by not paying. Now please don't misunderstand what I am saying here, I believe God is going to provide the funds for us to pay off these debts. I'm not implying that everyone should stop paying their bills. This is a "testing season" for us. Once we get through this test our Heavenly Father will take care of these bills for us. The important part to remember here is to not get yourself into these situations. Also keep in mind that God does test our faith in Him. This may require us to abandon our *natural* thought process in favor of His supernatural realm. I am exposing my errors in order to help people. *Please* use the worksheets at the end of this book to gain control of God's resources.

Chapter 5

Net Worth

Net worth is in the news all the time. The wealthy are judged by their *net worth*. My definition of *net worth* is: total *assets* minus total *liabilities*. A strong household or business will have a **2:1 ratio** of *assets* to *liabilities*. What this means is that at any given time your household should have twice the *assets* versus *liabilities*. As an example, if you have $500,000 in *assets*, your *liabilities* should be no more than $250,000. If this rule is used it will keep you from over-spending and getting in over your head with the *liabilities*. It is best to do a "financial check-up" every six months. It is also very important, to do a *net worth* evaluation before a big purchase, such as a bigger home, a vacation home, or third car, etc.

In the back of this book is a *net worth* evaluation sheet. I encourage people to use this in their quest to manage money according to the Kingdom of God.

I would like to talk about *cash flow*. At the end of this book, I have a worksheet for everyone to use for their *cash flow* evaluation. I look at a household as a business. A business has expenses: *fixed* and *variable*. A business also has *income* or *revenue*. A household has expenses and income. It only takes a few minutes to go through this sheet and plug the information into it. Once you have arrived at a total for the expense and income column, all you have to do is subtract the two totals from each other. This will tell you if your household is operating at a **loss** or **profit** for the month.

In the business world, if the losses continue month after month, the business will fail. Depending on the size of the company it may file for bankruptcy. If your household continues to lose money month after month, you will end up declaring bankruptcy too.

This is the reason it is so important to keep a budget. I have created these worksheets to make it very simple. I don't care if you want to use someone else's worksheet. The point is to write it down so that you have a good understanding of your finances. This is to help you manage God's resources.

One time I met with a young couple and they went through this worksheet and discovered they were operating at a **loss**. When this occurs there are really only two solutions: cut back expenses or increase income. My advice to them was to figure out where they could reduce their expenses. I prayed with them and left it at that. Months later, they told me that they were selling their house. I was shocked but excited for them at the same time.

This is what God had shown them to do about their **loss**. They sold their house and bought a less expensive one. In addition, they had extra money to pay off credit card debt. Since then, they had a baby and have gotten better jobs. Once they decided to make a *choice*, God was with them. One day God is going to give them a better house than they sold. The reason will be because they are managing His resources responsibly. God *wants* to bless us. He just *wants* to see us take care of what we have first. He is a great Father. In Psalms 115:14-15 "May the Lord give you increase more and more, You and your children. May you be blessed by the Lord, Who made heaven and earth."

Sunday $pending Instead of Sunday Giving

Chapter 6

Good/Bad Debt

Investments can be made with *good debt*. If we borrow money to make money that is *good debt*. Let's say we go to the bank and borrow money to buy a duplex or apartment building. This is a *debt*, but, we will make money from the money we borrowed through the rent payments coming in from the properties. In an early chapter, I explained how I borrowed money to purchase Ford stock. If I had paid back the money I borrowed then, I would have used *good debt* but instead it turned into *bad debt*. This is the most common mistake that we make with *debt*.

Most people think of *debt* as a bad word. It depends on how we use it. For example: most people might think guns are bad, but in reality it's the *choices* that people make who use the guns, not the guns themselves, that are bad. *Debt* is the same way. It depends on how we use the *debt*. *Debt* can work for us or against us. Guns can be used to hunt with or to hurt people. The **real choice** is ours. The government has laws and regulations in place to protect us from guns and *debt*. Just because the *choice* is there to use guns or debt does not give us the *right* to abuse them.

During the last real estate bubble, people would blame the bank for their debt problems, but the real problem was their lack of self control. We are all guilty of this at some point in our lives. Just because the bank approves us for $250,000 does not mean we have to purchase a home that cost that same amount. To be fair, I do believe people were taken advantage of for commission sales. As Kingdom people we must restrain from allowing our emotions to rule over principles. I believe more people need to be taught the basic principles of money management. This is the very reason I am taking the time to write this book. We as believers should not be taking advice from the world system, but they should be taking advice from us! In my first book "Who Is Your $ource," I explain how the world and kingdom systems differ. We should be using the world system to our advantage. Instead, some of the church is ensnared in the same *debt* trap as the people who do not know about the Kingdom principles. In Romans 8:12-14 "Therefore, brethren we are debtors-not to the flesh, to live according to the flesh. For if you live according to the flesh you will die; but if by the Spirit you put to death the deeds of the body, you will live. For as many as are led by the Spirit of God, these are the sons of God."

We cannot allow our emotions to affect us in financial decisions. This is allowing our **flesh** to rule over our Spirit. We should be asking the Holy Spirit for advice, not our emotions. Emotional buying is what gets some people into incredible financial trouble. Sometimes these shopping sprees are actually trying to fill a void in a person's life. It really is no different than an alcoholic or drug addict. We have to embrace the kingdom principles of managing money. We are to be the **lenders** not the borrowers. The only reason to borrow is to make more money. I have had two car loans in my entire life. I have no intention of getting anymore car loans. The best cars to drive are the ones that are paid for. I realize it is difficult to pay cash for a house but you could buy a less expensive house and use the extra money to invest. Then, later on down the road you can purchase a better home with more cash down from the money made from the investments. The problem some of us have with this idea is waiting. *Patience* is very important in financial decisions.

Choices are ultimately what shape our financial landscape. The daily *choices* we make affect our monthly and yearly budget. In order to keep debt under control, several *choices* need to be made:

1) *Listen*: Maintain an open mind when getting advice.
2) Gain *Knowledge*: Desire to understand more about your finances.

3) *Change*: Be willing to find better alternatives for your finances.

4) *Discipline*: Stick with the budget.

5) *Sacrifice*: Give up purchases now for better opportunities later.

6) Exercise *Patience*: Wait for the right time to buy.

7) *Persevere*: Endure the wait believing you will reach your goals.

8) Protect *Credit*: Protect your credit score.

9) *Walk in Self control*: Be led by the Spirit not the flesh.

10) *Walk in Integrity*: Don't compromise your future.

Chapter 7

$ Working for You

The best way to enjoy financial freedom is to have your money working for you. It is best to have at least *five* different income streams. For instance, my wife and I have some property and that gives us monthly income. Second, we have residual income from the books that I write and sell. Third, we will have income from Ju'bilee Tea that I co-founded with two other guys. The fourth one is a company with a product called Flippee that my wife and I will be purchasing soon. The fifth one is a project I'm working on; Koozie Kompany with a product called Fountain Friend.

These companies are very different from each other. It is good to have diversity. This will ensure that when one business is down, another will be up. The days of relying on your job as your only income are over. All it takes is one bad day at your job and your income goes to zero overnight. I know, because shortly after my wife Bethany and I were married we both lost our jobs. We have sustained ourselves with the income from the properties and some supernatural intervention from heaven.

I have searched high and low for all types of different business ideas. I am the type of person that is always looking for an opportunity. A few things I have learned are: the good ones have a small amount of start-up capital required; consumable products are best; and it's best that the businesses don't require a lot of time. Time is the most valuable resource we posses.

When it comes to investments, the real question should be, "how much time are you willing to put into the investment?" For me, in the beginning, I thought that no matter how much time I put into a project it would be successful. I am a very determined individual and a workaholic. The problem with this philosophy is that I'm trying to do it all by myself. I have learned over the years that doing business/investments in the "natural" requires a lot of time. Also, the outcome may not be what you had anticipated. If we will let the Holy Spirit guide us and co-labor with Him, we will get much better results. In the Supernatural, God can create amazing opportunities with very little effort on our part. The **key** to this success is focusing on Him and not the project or opportunity. I am just now starting to understand this at 42 years of age. It is never too late to get started.

God does not want us working so much that we cannot do the work of the Kingdom. It has been challenging for me to write these books. I know that this is a part of the ministry that God wants me to do for His Kingdom. If I will settle into this role, then He will begin to open doors of opportunity for me. God always wants to bless His children. What He is waiting for is *our* obedience.

    I have realized over the years that some of my property investments have taken up a lot of time. I was working a full time job and working on properties too. I am thankful for all those years of hard work because my wife and I are living off of them. I can't help but wonder if maybe there was an easier path that I could have taken, but could not see it. This is really important to remember. Sometimes, we get inside of a project and have tunnel vision. I have begun to realize that opportunities can come from anywhere. We just need to stay in tune with the Holy Spirit. Here are some of the best investments:

1)   *Kingdom*: Sow resources of time, talent or money into ministries /charitable organizations or your local church.
2)   *People*: help others get to their destination and God will send help for you to get to your destiny.
3)   *Yourself*: Read books, magazines and the Bible. Watch inspiring movies, documentaries, and teachings. Create time for yourself.
4)   *Family*: Promote their dreams. Encourage them to succeed. Support them in their projects. This will help you when you need encouragement.

God's Kingdom is based on: **other people first, and we are second**. It is also based on *love*. We love other people and it will come back to us. This might be a different investment strategy than the world's, but I can guarantee you that it will work. People always want the easy way to success. The Kingdom way is not easy, but it sure is adventurous. Invest in the Kingdom… it's a sure winner!

Chapter 8

You Working for $

I have a lot of experience in working for my money. I actually enjoyed working very hard for it. The problem with this philosophy is that I had no time to do the work of the Kingdom of God or anything else. This is exactly what the enemy wants us to do. It is one of his old tricks. Don't fall for it!

We get so consumed with our work that we don't know which way we are going. I remember working so many hours in a week that I would not have time to go to the grocery store to buy food. I would also eat out. This is not good for your body. I believed what I was doing was for the Kingdom of God. In other words, the money that was made by working, I was investing into the Kingdom. This is where the enemy can keep you on a path that looks right, but is actually taking you farther away from your God-given destiny.

Debt can cause the same results. We get ourselves into debt and the only way out is to work more than we did. This is how we become a slave to debt: just going to work every day to make it through another week. This is *not* how He wants us to live in the Kingdom. We are to look to our Father in heaven as our source. He will provide for us **if** we will do His work. I am beginning to understand how this works. For almost a year, my wife and I have not worked in secular jobs. Each day we wake up and spend time with our heavenly Father. I have a much better relationship with Him today. I have written three books in this time frame as well. I began to realize that if I will obey Him by writing these books, He will provide "supernatural" opportunities to create wealth. I am so blessed to be set free from the *rat race* of life. Believe me, it is a completely different way to live than what I have grown up to experience. Most of us think, *if we go to college, get a job and work real hard, everything will work out for us*. I'm here to tell you that the only way is God's way, *period*. If we do it *His* way we can earn *more* money doing *less* work, but we *must* put Him **first**. I am on this path and have no intentions of going back to my old way of doing things. It is really hard on my flesh, but once I get past that part, I know God will bless me in ways that I cannot even imagine. This is what he wants for all of His children, not just me. I encourage you today to take a leap of faith and get on the path to freedom in Him. God Bless!

Chapter 9

Sabbath Day

In Exodus 20:8-11 "Remember the Sabbath day, to keep it holy. Six days you shall labor and do all your work, but the seventh day is the Sabbath of the Lord your God. In it you shall do no work: you, nor your son, nor your daughter, nor your male servants, nor your female servants, nor your cattle, nor your stranger who is within your gates. For in six days the Lord made the heavens and the earth, the sea, and all that is in them, and rested on the seventh day. Therefore the Lord blessed the Sabbath day and hallowed it."

Also in Exodus when God was giving Moses instructions on how to gather the manna: Exodus 16:21-30 "So they gathered it every morning, every man according to his need. And when the sun became hot, it melted. And so it was, on the sixth day, that they gathered twice as much bread, two omers for each one. And all the rulers of the congregation came and told Moses. Then he said to them, "This is what the Lord has said: 'Tomorrow is a Sabbath rest, a holy Sabbath to the Lord. Bake what you will bake today, and boil what you will boil; and lay up for yourselves all that remains, to be kept until morning.'" So they laid it up till morning, as Moses commanded; and it did not stink, nor were there any worms in it. Then Moses said, "Eat that today, for today is a Sabbath to the Lord; today you will not find it in the field. Six days you shall gather it, but on the seventh day, the Sabbath, there will be none." Now it happened that some of the people went out on the seventh day to gather, but they found none. And the Lord said to Moses, "How long do you refuse to keep My commandments and My laws? "See! For the Lord has given you the Sabbath; therefore He gives you on the sixth day bread for two days. Let every man remain in his place; let no man go out of his place on the seventh day." So the people rested on the seventh day."

Here is the modern day revelation that God gave me as I was typing these scriptures into this book; If we go out on the *Sabbath* day and *spend* money we do not have, that becomes a *liability*. And remember a *liability* is any financial obligation, debt, claim or potential loss. So, I believe God is saying that spending money on the Sabbath is okay **if** we have the money to spend. On the other hand, if we are getting ourselves in debt, we are actually disobeying His commandment. Let me explain this a little deeper. The commandment says not to *work* on the

Sabbath day. Well, if we go into debt on the Sabbath day, we are actually *creating a liability* that we will have to work off later. I have never looked at this commandment from this perspective before in my life. This revelation is coming to me as I write this book. I will now have to incorporate this new revelation into my life. Also, spending money that we don't have may require us to work seven days a week to pay for everything. This would also be in violation of his commandment. In order for God to bless us, we must *obey* His commandments.

Sunday $pending Instead of Sunday Giving

Chapter 10

Tithing

My definition of *tithing*: returning a portion of the resources back to the owner. You notice I did not put a percent in my definition. The reason is very simple: I am trying to encourage **everyone** to *tithe*. Some people may not be able to *tithe* 10% back to the Creator when they first start giving. *I want to encourage everyone to give something.* The amount is not important. God looks at the heart of the giver not the amount of the gift. The church gets too hung up on percentages. This can turn into religion. God does not want giving to be religious.

In my work sheet at the back of this book, I have *tithe* (Kingdom Tax) as 10% of all your after-tax income. A tax is something that is required to pay for the services received from that entity. In our case, God wants us to pay Him a mere 10% tax for all the resources that flow through our hands. Now, keep in mind the resources come from Him and that is the reason for the tax. That is what I believe it should be. I know that people will get into arguments about after or before taxes giving. This is ridiculous because God does not want us to stop at 10%. This is merely a **starting point**. And for those who can't start at 10%, just start giving whatever amount you can and He will bless you. Then, as God begins to bless you, increase your tithe. And before you know it, He will have blessed you so much that you are tithing 10% or more. Some people of the body of Christ have a hard time understanding this revelation. We are to go beyond the 10%. I hope to one day be able to give at least 50% of my income away. I am not there yet but I am beyond the standard 10%.

A *tithe* (Kingdom Tax) is for our benefit not God's. He already has all the resources He will ever need. The point to tithing is for us to acknowledge that the resources we posses are from Him. We are merely managers of God's resources. I look at tithing a little different than some people. We cannot out-give the Creator of the universe because His word tells us that in 2 Corinthians 9:6 "But this I say: He who sows sparingly will also reap sparingly, and he who sows bountifully will also reap bountifully." So God owns everything because He created everything.

You will also notice on the worksheet that *tithe* is **first** on the fixed expense sheet. I put that there so we can remember that *tithing* is just like any other bill, **except it is always paid first**. Earlier I mentioned that my wife and I had to make a decision about not paying some credit card bills. *I still pay my tithe*. I will tell you one reason why: it's the only way to get out of the test we are currently experiencing. If I stop *tithing* then I will cut-off the source that can pay all my debts off in one day. That might sound *crazy* to some people but that is where faith comes into action. He expects us to have faith with our works! Never under estimate the power of giving!

Tithing is the only guaranteed investment you will ever find with a 100% plus rate of return. I have people ask me, "Where should I invest my money?" My response is always "The Kingdom of God". It is the safest and best place to put your money. The problem we have with this Kingdom principle is the harvest time. We have no idea when it will come, and that makes it difficult for us to see it. This is when we have to use our faith. God is always on time. As I write this book, my wife and I are believing for a huge **breakthrough** in our finances. I know it will come because we have sown a lot of seed. If we do not sow seed we will not reap a harvest. This is why it is so important to *give* **something/anything** as a *tithe* (Kingdom Tax) to God. I pray that if you only learn one thing from this book, it is this: **tithing is not an option. It is a necessity. It is your very life-line to God.** Happy tithing!!!!!!!!!!!!!!

Sunday $pending Instead of Sunday Giving

Kingdom Financial Plan
"Prosperity Begins With Investments"™

Ten Successful Prosperity Choices™

Listen: Maintain an open mind.

Knowledge: Desire increased understanding.

Change: Consider beneficial alternatives.

Discipline: Commit to the plan of success.

Sacrifice: Embrace "short-term cost" for "long-term gain" strategy.

Patience: Wait for planned results.

Perseverance: Endure initial discomfort with focus on accomplished goal(s).

Good Credit: Build/protect high credit score by making on-time payments.

Self Control: Keep emotions in check, avoid poor financial decisions.

Integrity: Avoid compromise, adhere to the Kingdom Principles.

Kingdom Financial Plan™

1) **Manage:** Direct resources in a responsible manner.
2) **Tithe:** Return a portion of the resources back to the owner.
3) **Invest:** Sacrifice today for tomorrow's opportunities.

Manage: Develop a reasonable resources allocation plan. Diligently spend resources on needs, not wants. Never spend resources that you do not have.

Tithe: Tithe (Kingdom Tax) 10% of **all** your after-taxes income to your local church.

Invest: Develop a reasonable resources allocation plan for investing the **Profits** (surplus of resources) from your corporation, small business, household, and/or not-for-profit into your home, family, self, other people, and the Kingdom.

Manage + Tithe + Invest = Kingdom Financial Plan™

Kingdom Tax101™

Failing to plan is planning to fail. If we do not plan to tithe, we plan to not tithe. Tithes should be paid like any other liability we owe, only first. A tithe is a Kingdom Tax that everyone is required to pay similar to income taxes. The tithing principle teaches that prosperity is not of our own doing. We reap from what we have sown in the appropriate time of harvest. Paying our Kingdom taxes in an acceptable manner assures us of a good future harvest. Give and you shall receive, pressed down, shaken together, and running over. Applying faith with ones tithe always yields rich dividends.

"Prosperity Begins With Investments"™

Net Worth Evaluation

Assets: Any items of economic value owned by an individual or corporation, especially that which could be converted to cash.

Liabilities: Any financial obligations, debts, claims, or potential losses.

ASSETS		LIABILITIES	
Cash	$	Home Mortgage	$
401k	$	Auto Loan(s)	$
Roth IRA	$	Credit Card(s)	$
Real Estate	$	Other Loan(s)	$
Home	$	Other Mortgage(s)	$
Auto	$	Student Loan(s)	$
Stocks & Bonds	$	Life Insurance	$
Total Assets	$	**Total Liabilities**	$
Total Net Worth	$		

Net Worth is total Assets minus total Liabilities. A strong financial corporation, small business, household or not-for-profit will have a **2:1 Ratio** of Assets to Liabilities.

"Prosperity Begins With Investments"™

Kingdom Management101™

FIXED EXPENSES			
Tithe	$	Life insurance	$
Food	$	Car payment(s)	$
Rent/Mortgage	$	Gas	$
Gas & Electric	$	Child care	$
Water, Sewer & Trash	$	Student loan(s)	$
Property taxes	$	Credit card(s)	$
Child Support	$	Other loan(s)	$
Health insurance	$	Household supplies	$
Home insurance	$	Phone & Internet	$
Car insurance	$	Cable / Satellite TV	$
Subtotal	$	**Subtotal**	

VARIABLE EXPENSES		INCOME	
Clothing	$	Primary	$
Medical	$	Secondary	$
Education (k-12)	$	Investments	$
Car maintenance	$	Other	$
Home maintenance	$		
Legal	$		
Vacations	$		
Entertainment	$		
Hobbies	$	**TOTAL INCOME**	$
Miscellaneous	$	**TOTAL EXPENSE**	$
Subtotal	$	**PROFIT OR LOSS**	$

"Prosperity Begins With Investments"™

Kingdom Investments101™

Investment: Prepare for future opportunities.

Home Improvements: 2:1 rule - Two dollars of increased home value for each dollar spent.

Roth IRA: $1,000.00 per year minimum investment.

401(K): Max out employer's matching funds.

College Fund: Invest in a State 529 Plan.

Stocks: Invest 75% with 10% - 25% in foreign stocks.

Bonds: Invest 25% in Treasury Inflation-Protected Securities (TIPS).

Money Market: Park cash here when waiting for good investment opportunity.

Real Estate: Buy at 10% - 15% below market value (consider market trends).

Kingdom: Sow into other ministries / charitable donations.

People: Help others in need.

Yourself: Invest in teachings (books, CDs, DVDs, etc.) that enhance personal growth.

Family: Promote dreams of loved ones.

Real Estate Investment Evaluation

Income to Debt Ratio: Minimum of 20% Return on Investment (ROI).

    Example: $10,000 minimum gross income from a $50,000 loan.

Purchase Price: Buy at a minimum of 10% below market value.

    Example: $50,000 market value should be purchased at $45,000 or less.

Carrying Costs: Include in total investment cost.

    Example: Accrued property taxes on vacant land until sold.

Fixed Costs: Include in total investment cost.

    Example: Mortgage payments, loan interest, utilities, insurance, HOA, etc.

Variable Costs: Include in total investment cost.

    Example: One time permit fees, ongoing maintenance, etc.

Sunday $pending Instead of Sunday Giving

Contact the Author

Kevin L. Cann

Kingdom Management & Investments, LLC

Email:
kevincann@kingdommanagement101.com

Website: www.kingdommanagement101.com

Sunday $pending Instead of Sunday Giving

Other Products Available

KEVIN L. CANN'S book is about the world's system of earth and the Kingdom system of Heaven. Today, many people do not understand the Kingdom system and that is because we are taught the world's system. God wants us to understand how His Kingdom system works so we can manifest it on earth. We will learn how to bring heaven to earth through the Kingdom system. That's how we know that GOD IS OUR SOURCE.

God ways are not our ways and HIS thoughts are not our thoughts. More of HIM.... Less of Me by **MARK KRENNING** explains how God has revealed himself to me. How HE has used what was meant for my destruction to bring me closer to HIM and how HE has given me a deeper revelation of what was accomplished through Jesus' life, death, and resurrection.

Available Everywhere Books Are Sold

www.ingramcontent.com/pod-product-compliance
Lightning Source LLC
Chambersburg PA
CBHW072110290426
44110CB00014B/1882